# Python

A book for beginners that is able to accommodate
intermediate and more advanced programmers

Note: Some words or numbers are highlighted to indicate that
they are referring to the code or programming language. These
highlighted words or numbers may not make sense in a sentence
unless read carefully.

# Introduction

I would like to thank you for purchasing the book, Understanding Python, a guide to learn Python for all.

With the advent of e book culture, we witness that there is a huge amount of material on every topic imaginable printed every day. It becomes quite cumbersome for the reader to choose what is good for them and what will really provide what the title promises and what does not.

Especially on the subject of Information Technology, Software development and web development, you will find books upon books each claiming to make you an expert in its respective field within minutes of purchase.

Here we make no such claim. This book contains proven steps and strategies on how to understand and completely learn the language Python. But like other tools and languages the key to learn it is not in just reading the book but to get hands on experience by practicing the code that is given in examples as well as practice on your own. We have given many examples, feel free to change them as you like. The more you practice the more you will learn. Think of new ideas that can enhance your code and make it more useful. For example, if you have been given an example that will take two numbers and find their sum, try to write code for the same function of three numbers or more.

Another important thing that my readers should know is that this book is aimed at beginners but it accommodates intermediate and more advanced programmers. I assume three types of readers would be interested in this book. Those who have no knowledge about programming and this is their first venture in the world of software development. Secondly those who know programming and want to increase their software development skills by learning a new language, Python. And thirdly who understand Python and have worked with it and are interested in the book just to increase their knowledge of the language.

This book caters to all three kinds of readers. For the first type of reader in each chapter when a new concept of the language is introduced some general background is given that will explain the concept before going into the specifications of the concept with regards to Python. Here it is highly recommended to the readers that they search for other online resources to clarify and strengthen their concepts.

The second type of reader can skip the introductory explanation of the concept in each chapter and resume from the Python specifications of each concept. And the third kind of reader can skip the first few chapters altogether and go to the higher concepts directly. However, in this book we cover from the basics to string operations, functions and loops. For higher concepts consult books on advanced Python concepts.

Thanks again for downloading this book, I hope you enjoy it!

# Contents

# CHAPTER 1

# A LITTLE ABOUT COMPUTERS AND PROGRAMMING

# Chapter 1

# A Little about Computers and Programming

Today computers are everywhere. Offices, homes, schools, departmental stores, everywhere we look, we find computers in one form or the other. In today's world there is no escaping the use of these machines. We use them to search for information, performing complex calculations, storing data, paying bills, human capital optimizations etc. Why these machines are so popular? The answer is simple and straight forward. Computers help us in day to day life, they make things easier and straight forward for us.

However, on their own these machines are unable to do anything. People tell them exactly what to do and they follow the instructions. These instructions that tell computers what to do are called computer programs and people who write these programs are called computer programmers or software engineers.

## 1.1 What is programming?

Now as we have established that computers follow instructions, the question arises how do we make computers understand what we want to tell them and in what language do we give the computers instructions.

Computers understand instructions written in special languages. Programs that are written in these languages give computers an exact sequence of steps to follow and the computer will follow these instructions without questioning or asking anything. Here we must mention that in our everyday life many times we give instructions to fellow human beings but we take certain things for granted thinking that people will automatically do some in between steps. For example, if a teacher asks a student sitting in his classroom to bring a book from the library he will give a single line instruction to bring such and such book from the library. However, there are several intermediate steps involved to carry out this instruction. The following sequence give the exact detail about how to carry out this instruction.

1. Stand up from the chair.

2. Go out of the class room.

3. Turn left.

4. When you reach the library ask permission to enter.

5. Look for the book in the respective section.

6. Pull out the book.

7. Check out the book by informing the librarian.

8. Go back to the classroom.

9. Handover the book to the teacher.

Hence you see that a single one line instruction requires a detailed process that we do not need to explain to people because they already know the intermediate steps but the case is different with computers. We have to tell them every single detail. Even in this case there may be some scenarios when the computer would block out our working because we have omitted the details like what if the book is not on the shelf or what if the librarian does not grant the student permission to enter the library. These small details are what we need to cater to while writing computer programs because computers do not have insight like humans. They cannot make any decisions like if one book is not available take another one that is similar to the one required, which can serve the same purpose. We make decisions for the computers. A good computer program will look for all the arcs what might stem from a decision point and write instructions for each case. The instructions are written in special computer understandable languages called programming languages.

## 1.2 Types of programming languages

There are numerous languages in which programmers write the instructions or code that would make computers do useful tasks. One might argue that why is there not one single language that tells the computer to do different tasks which could save the programmers from the hassle of learning so many different languages. The truth is that the computer understands everything by breaking it into a singular machine understandable binary code.

With the advancement in technology there are so many different ways in which we can program our machines and get benefit from them. Different languages are written keeping in view certain functionalities. However, recently languages are written keeping in mind ease of learning for the programmers. Such that programmers may feel like giving out instructions in the same way as to any other fellow human. This makes programming much easier.

There are three groups in which we can divide the computer languages.

## 1.2.1 High level programming languages

High level languages are similar to normal human languages. They are easier to understand and to program in.

languages like C, C++, COBOL, fall in this category while our case study PYTHON is also a high level programming language. A program written in high level language is called a source code. A computer cannot understand the source code by itself. It needs special programs that translates the source code into machine understandable instructions. A compiler is a program that translates a high level language into a machine code. To the compiler a source program is just input data. The output that it generates against the input is called an object program. Object program is the machine language version of the program. However, a **compiler** needs an entire file of source code and it parses it as a whole, on the other hand an **interpreter** is another translator program that parses the source code line by line. Python is an interpreter program and does not follow the boilerplate model.

The main advantage of code written in high level language is that it is portable. It can run on any machine given that the machine has a proper compiler program that understands the specific source code.

## 1.2.2 Low Level Programming Language

A low level programming language is closer to machine code. Here instructions are represented as mnemonics. For example, typical instructions for addition and subtraction would look like following in a low level language like Assembly language.

ADD

SUB

Although languages like assembly is a difficult, it gives users more power to manipulate the machine according to his requirements. An assembler is a program that is used to translate instructions written in assembly language and convert it to machine code.

## 1.2.3 Machine Language

The language made up of binary coded instructions that is used directly by the computer is called machine language code. When computers were first developed the only programming language available was the primitive instruction set built into each machine called the machine code. The machine code is not similar on every computer.

In a computer data is represented electronically by pulses of electricity. Electrical circuits in their simplest form are either on or off. Usually a circuit that is on is represented by 1 and a circuit that is off is represented by 0. Any kind of data can be represented by combinations of 0's and 1's. We simply have to choose which combination represents each piece of information. The process of assigning bit patterns to pieces of data is called coding.

The word bit that will often be used in programming refers to a single 0 or 1. A group of four bits is called a nibble. It is a pattern of 0's and 1's in a group of fours, but nibbles are very seldom used nowadays. A byte is a group of 8 bits. It can represent 2 to the power of 8 that is 256 combinations. In a computer each character is represented by a byte. However, now 8 bit computers are being replaced by 16 or 32 bit computers.

Working with binary combinations is a tedious process and fortunately nowadays we no longer work in it. Instead we use high level languages like Python with a language translator that would convert our instructions into machine code.

## 1.3 Phases of programming

Now that we have come to know about what computer programs are and how they are written, let us learn the process of writing a computer program. A computer program should be written in a systematic sequence of steps.

It all starts with a problem. We are given a situation and we have to find a programmable solution to it. it involves basically three main phases.

### 1.3.1 Problem solving phase

- Analysis and specification of the problem

- Developing an algorithm or sequence of steps to the solution.

- Verification of the algorithm.

### 1.3.2 Implementation Phase

- Translating the algorithm into a program.

11

- Testing the program for various test cases.

### 1.3.3 Maintenance Phase

- Using the program by end users.

- Modify the program according to the changing requirements and correct any errors that may occur.

Now let us discuss a little detail about algorithms. The process of writing a program begins by analyzing the problem and developing a general solution called an algorithm. It is highly advisable to spend a good amount of time analyzing the problem and developing the right algorithm before actually implementing the solution. This will ultimately save time and save a lot of effort later. Although a person is usually tempted to start writing the code immediately, in the long run it will end up in developing an erroneous code and would require a lot of time and effort to identify the errors and fix the bugs.

An algorithm is a step by step procedure for solving a problem in a finite amount of time. Translating an algorithm into a programming language is called coding the algorithm. The product of this translation is called a program. Running this program on a computer is called an execution. During the execution a number of errors and bugs can occur. That is when we use the concept of debugging. Debugging is basically tracking and removing errors from a program.

After a program is successfully executed and deployed on a computer machine it proceeds to the maintenance phase. In this phase whenever errors are reported by the client by testing with the real data, it needs to be fixed by modifying the program. A nicely written program that follows the general rules and good programming practices is easy to modify and update. That is why it is highly advisable to write the program following all the good practices that will be mentioned in this book as we move on to the next chapters.

Maintenance is also required once the requirements change or data is modified. For example, the program for a supermarket must provide provisions for an increase in the number of the items, changing prices, updates in sales tax.

Now that we are familiar with the general concepts, let us move on to learning about Python.

# Summary

We learnt the following concepts in this chapter.

- A process of planning and developing a sequence of steps for the computer to follow is known as computer programming.

- An algorithm is a step by step process for solving a problem in a finite amount of time.

- A set of rules, symbols and special words used to construct a program is called a programming language.

- Translating an algorithm into a programming language is called coding the algorithm.

- Binary code or machine code are combination of 0's and 1's that represent instructions.

- A program written in high level language is called source code while a program written in binary is called machine code.

- Compilers and interpreters are used to translate source code into machine code. Python is an interpreter based language.

# CHAPTER 2

# HISTORY OF PYTHON AND INSTALLATION

# Chapter 2
# History of Python and installation

The recent trend in newly developed programming languages is to make them as easy and understandable as possible. It is fast becoming popular that programming should not be just the prerogative of software engineers but everyone should be able to write simple programs. This is mainly to manage the computers in their field in the best possible way.

Python is one such high level language that is easy to grasp. It uses a relatively small set of keywords to carry out instructions and commands. Keywords or reserved words are words that have a preset and definite meaning in a language. It cannot mean anything else. Whenever a keyword is written in a source code the compiler will always do the one operation as instructed. (A complete list of reserved words used in Python is given at the end of this chapter.)

For example, the most commonly used keyword in Python is 'print'. It is used to do exactly what it literally means, to print something. So if we write

Print 'Hello World'

On a machine where Python is installed and we are on the correct command prompt, on pressing enter Hello World will be printed. Here there is one small detail that needs to be kept in view and that is only Hello World will be printed and quotes are not included. Whatever we want to print needs to be enclosed in quotes and that comes under the syntax of the language. We will learn more about syntax and semantics of the language later in the chapter. First let us get to know a little about history of Python language.

## 2.1 History of Python

Python was developed in 1989, by Guido Van Rossum. He developed it as a hobby project, to keep busy durinh Christmas holidays, without having long term plans about how to take it further. It was originally developed to appeal to C and unix hackers however it became quite popular because of its simplicity and ease of use. In Python we can do tasks in fewer lines of code as compared to languages like C++ and java.

Python is a high level language that supports a number of software development paradigms like object oriented, structural or multi paradigm. Its name is derived from the famous television series Monty Python's Flying circus. It was favorite show of Van Rossum so he named his creation after it.

Two main versions of Python are being used these days, Python 2 and Python 3. Python 2 was launched in October 2000 and it introduced major changes and updates making the language more adaptable and added new features. In December 2008 Python 3 was released which was majorly backward incompatible.

The main philosophy of Python is given by five statements in the document The Zen of Python

- Beautiful is better than ugly.

- Explicit is better than implicit.

- Simple is better than complex

- Complex is better than complicated.

- Readability counts.

It is a highly extensible language and the functionality is not written in the core. Instead a huge library is added that includes the features and new features can be added as well.

Since 2003 Python has been included in the list of top ten programming languages. In 2016 it was ranked at number 5. Twice it has been awarded the programming language of the year award. It is widely used in large organizations like Google, CERN, and Nasa. The popular site Reddit is completely written in Python. It is among many other sites that make use of this programming language.

## 2.2 Installing Python on your machines

Before you can start writing programs in Python you first need to install it on your machines. In order to develop programs, you need two things, firstly a text editor to write programs in and secondly a language translator that will change our source code into binary instructions or machine code that the computer can then directly execute.

In order to download Python, go to www.Python.org/downloads/. There you can select the latest version of Python 2 according to the specifications of your machine. In this book we are using Python 2 as a standard for all of the examples. You are welcome to use Python 3 also but please Google the differences between Python 2 and Python 3. Thereafter, update the code given in examples according to that.

Windows and Machintosh are two of the most widely used operating systems available and we will discuss in detail about installing Python on both of these.

## 2.2.1 Installing Python on Windows

On windows MS word and Notepad are the most commonly used text editors but they are NOT recommended to write Python or other programs in. Source code should be written in flat text editor that does not insert extra bytes to the code like Word or Notepad. Instead Notepad++ is a good editor for people using Windows to write their code in. another great option is Sublime text editor. Sublime shows the code in colored patterns that makes detecting syntactical mistakes and errors easier.

Install Python on your machines by selecting the correct version from www.Python.org/downloads/. Once it is installed a folder will be created in the C drive of your computer by the name of Python27 or whichever version you have downloaded. You can download Python into any folder on your computer but make sure to set up the path correctly.

If you already have text editors like Notepad++ or sublime then great, otherwise you can download them for free from www.notepad-plus-plus.org and www.sublimetext.com.

Once the text editor and Python are both installed on your computer, you can start writing the programs. Let us go through step by step instructions of how to run the Python program.

1. Open the text editor and write a simple one line program print 'Hello World'

2. Save the text file with extension of .py. For example, first create a folder on desktop named Python, then we save the file on our desktop folder Python with name myFirstProgram.py.

3. Open the command prompt. It will open with your default directory path set.

4. Write cd desktop and press enter, to go to the place where we have stored the file.

5. Type cd Python and press enter. To check whether you have reached the correct path write dir (displays all the files in the directory), if your file

name appears in the list then you are in the right folder.

6. In order to execute the file just write the name of the file myFirstProgram.pg on the command prompt and press enter. Hello World will be printed on the screen.

## 2.2.2 Installing Python for Mackintosh

The requirements to run Python on Mac are similar to those on Windows however the good news here is that Python is built in the Mac OS so you just need a good text editor to write your programs in. Here the recommended text editor is TextWrangler. You can download this text editor from www.barebones.com for free. Do not try to write source code in TextEdit, as it adds extra string to the code making it impossible for the Python interpreter to understand it properly. Following steps will guide you in running a simple Python program on Mac machines successfully.

1. Create a folder on your desktop with the name Python to contain all the files containing source code. You can make the folder anywhere but you should know the full path of the folder.

2. Open the test editor and create a file with extension .py. Let us suppose the name of our file is myFirstProg.py and it contains a single line of code

   Print 'Hello World'

3. Save the file and the open the terminal program. The easiest way to do this is to press the spot light icon on the upper right corner and type terminal. Launch the application that pops up.

4. Terminal will be launched set to your default directory. We have to go to the directory where our file is located.

5. Write cd desktop and press enter to go to the desktop folder.

6. Then write cd Python to reach the folder where our source code file is located.

7. To execute the code just write the name of the file on command prompt and press enter.

8. The screen will show Hello World and you know that your code works.

Here it is important to know that setting up a development environment and making it work is often a tedious task and can take a few trials until a proper working environment is reached. The key is not to lose heart and keep on trying. First we have written a single line code to test the work environment. Once the development environment is set up you are ready to write more complicated programs.

In both Notepad++ and TextWrangler check the preferences and set the expand text to four spaces. It will save you a lot of time and effort and you can easily do the correct indentation for Python programs. More about indentation and Python program structure is in the next chapter.

# Summary

We learnt the following concepts in this chapter

- Keywords or reserved words have special and definite meaning in the language.

- Python is a high level language that is similar to common conversation.

- Python was developed in 1989 and now different versions of Python 2 and Python 3 are being used.

- Python can be used on Windows and Mac systems by installing it from official Python site.

- To write Python code use flat text editors like Notepad++ for windows and TextWrangler for Mac.

# Complete list of PYTHON keywords

| And | del | from | not | while |
| As | elif | global | or | with |
| assert | else | if | pass | yield |
| break | except | import | print | class |
| exec | in | raise | continue | finally |
| is | return | def | for | lamda |
| try | | | | |

# Chapter 3

# Starting with syntax of Python

# Chapter 3

# Starting with Syntax of Python

Now we begin with the explanation of a word that we've been using for quite some time. The syntax of a language is basically the grammar of the language. It means to write the language properly. The formal rules governing how valid instructions are written in a programming language that determines exactly what combinations of letters, numbers and symbols can be used in a program is basically syntax. There is no room for error or ambiguity in the syntax of the language because as mentioned computers cannot think on their own. They will do what it is told so it needs to be given the correct instructions. For example, when we are providing the print instructions we cannot write Print or PRINT. It has to be print written in small letters because that is what Python interpreter had been told to learn to understand. Writing it in any other way would just send an error message.

As compared to syntax is the semantics of the language. Semantics are the set of rules that determine the meaning of instructions written in a programming language. While syntax is checked by the interpreter at the time of execution of the program, mistakes in the semantics of the program are usually harder to detect. To avoid semantic mistakes, it is advised to spend time on planning and analysis of the problem before starting to code it. If planned properly, the program will have fewer logical and semantical mistakes and thus the implementation will take much less time.

An example of mistake in the semantics of the language is when we calculate the mean of different numbers. Instead of dividing the sum of numbers with the (total number) if we divide it with (total number)-1 the result would be wrong but the interpreter would not show any errors because it does not understand the semantics of the programs, the programmer has to take care of it.

Now let us take a look at various parts of a Python program. Unlike compiler based languages, an interpreter based language does not need a complete program before it can parse it. It can take a single line of code and interpret it for the computer.

## 3.1 Values and variables

Value is the basic unit used in a source code. For example, in the code print 'Hello World' the value is Hello world. Here are some more code examples to illustrate the meaning of values.

X=4

message = 'I am a sentence.'

y = 3.2425646

In the above examples 4, I am a sentence and 3.2425646 are all types of values. Values do not exist independently. They are assigned to some variable like in the above examples X, message and y are all names of variables. The main power of a programming language lies in its ability to define variables, performing operations on them and updating them. There are different types of variables. The type of variable depends upon the data or value that it is assigned to. Now 'X' has the value of 4 so it is an integer. The variable 'Message' has stored a string in it that reads I am a sentence so it is a string variable. 'Y' is a special type of variable that stores long decimal numbers. It is called a floating point variable. In order to perform long numerical operations that require results in a long number of digits after decimal point floating point variables are used. Now consider these examples.

x = '2'

v = '3.14'

here the value of x and v is 2 and 3.14 respectively but it is not considered as a numerical value falling in the category of integer and floating point. As the numbers are enclosed in quotes, they are considered as strings. If you want to apply string operations on the numbers save them in quotes. This is relevant where numbers come within addresses like house numbers, street numbers or area codes.

Another type of variable that is commonly used is the Boolean variable. The Boolean variables can take only two values true and false. They are used to check conditions.

check = true

If (check == 'true')

print 'this is a sample.'

Here check is a Boolean variable that can be set to true or false.

## 3.2 Variable names

As we have seen variables are used by the program to remember certain values. In order to remember the value, it is given a special name called variable name. there are certain rules to define variable names.

We cannot use reserved words to define a variable name as reserved words already have definite meaning. If a reserved word is used as a variable name it will give an error. Programmers can give variables any name but it is advisable to give meaningful names that covey the correct reference to the value stored in the variable. For example, if we have to store names and addresses of people it is advisable that we store it in a variable with the label name and address instead of x, y or any other meaningless word. Although the language gives you freedom to use any word as a variable name but we have to remember that when you are working on a large project with many other people your code must be understandable and readable to everyone.

Variable names can contain letters and numbers but it is illegal to start a variable name with a number. A digit can come between the letters in the variable name or at the end but not at the start. The letter in the name can be uppercase and lower case but again it is good practice not to begin the name with capital letter.

The variable names should not have special characters or spaces. Only an underscore is allowed and that to separate words within a variable name. For example, to write studentname we can write student_name for clarity and readability. Here are some examples of invalid variable names.

45number

#code

Lambda

Student name

3452

In all of the above cases the variable names are invalid for different reasons. In first case 45number the variable name starts with a number. In the second case special character # is in the name. In the third case lambda is not allowed because it is a part of Python's reserved words list. In the case of student name, a space is included in the name which is not allowed. Lastly a numeric name is not allowed because the first letter has to be an alphabet.

In short variable names there can be both uppercase and lowercase alphabets, the special character underscore and digits from 0-9. Remember that the first letter of the name cannot be a number.

## 3.3 Statements and Script

A single line of code is known as a statement. There are many types of statements in Python. The most common type of statement is the print statement.

```
x = 5
```

```
print x
```

This example has two statements. This will print number 5 on screen. The first is the assignment statement that assigns value to the variable x. The next is the print statement that will print the value stored in the variable x on the screen. A Python interpreter can execute a statement or a sequence of statements, called a script. A script may be a combination of many different kinds of statements. When a script is given to an interpreter it will execute it line by line and give the result after interpreting each line of the script.

## 3.4 Operators and Operands

You might be wondering why special characters are not allowed in variable names. The reason is that many of the special characters are used to denote arithmetic operations in the language like addition, subtraction and multiplication. For example, + represents the addition operation and – represents subtraction, * is for multiplication and division is denoted by / (backslash).

The special characters that represent mathematical operations are called operators and the variables on which they perform these operations are called operands.

2-1

3+45

2*4

8/2

These functions will give the results 1, 48, 8 and 4 respectively. One important thing to note about the division operator is that it performs floor division. If we do 3/2 it will not be 1.5 but 1. The reason is that if both numbers are integers the answer would be an integer. If the numbers are floating point then the answer would be a decimal number.

Two other operators that are commonly used are ** used for exponentiation and % called the modulus operator. The modulus operator is used to find the remainder in the integer division. For example,

7/3 is 2 and 7%3 is 1. Usually in integer division both the division operator and the modulus operator are used together to get the quotient and the remainder.

The combinations of variables, values and operators is known as expressions. Variables and values alone are also known as expressions. So all the following three are expressions.

x

2

2 + x

If the interpreter is in a line by line mode a single line expression is evaluated and its result is printed on screen but if it is given as a part of whole script the result needs to be printed to be shown on screen.

## 3.5 Complex expressions and rules of precedence

Arithmetic operations are an integral part of computer programs. Highly complex mathematical expressions can be easily evaluated through single line code. However, the main thing here is to understand the precedence of each operation within the expression. Expressions must be formed taking great care that everything is in the proper order. Python interpreter follows the PEMDAS rules of precedence.

1. Parenthesis has the highest precedence. You can force an expression to work your way by enclosing the part you want to work out first within parenthesis. For example (4-2)*3 is 6 and (4+4)*4 is 32.

2. Second in the line of precedence is the exponent operator. 2**3*2 is 16 and 3**2+2 is 11. Here it is advisable to write the expressions like (2**3)*2 and (3**2+2). Although the answers are same but parentheses increase the readability and makes the user get to the result easily.

3. Multiplication and division operators have equal amount of precedence and their order depends upon their position in the expression. The precedence order is from left to right.

4. Addition and subtraction have the same precedence after the multiplication and division operators. Here again the left to right rule is

observed to find the right sequence of execution of the expression.

The following are some expressions. Try to find their result on your own first and then look at the result that we have written later. Its order of precedence might seem a little confusing at first, that is why it is a good idea to use parenthesis.

3+1+4-3

4*3+5-2

7/3+6

4+6-3

The expressions result to 5, 15, 8 and 7 respectively.

## 3.6 String Operations

Up till now we have studied numerical operations however there are some operations available on string variable also. The most commonly used string operation is the concatenation operation. This operation will combine two strings together. In

Python the +operator is overloaded to perform the string operation directly.

first_name = 'Bill'

last_name = 'Murray'

full_name = first_name+last_name

print full_name

this will print Bill Murray on the screen. For numerical string data the result is the same concatenation.

num1 = '34'

num2 = '43'

result = num1 +num2

,print result

here the result will be 3443.

## 3.7 Comments

Comments are an integral part of code. In software engineering a program comprises of thousands of lines of code and hundreds of people work on it simultaneously. It is a tedious task to understand the code written by someone else. That is when comments come in handy. Comments are remarks made by the programmers explaining the working of the code in simple language.

In Python the comments start with the symbol #. When Python interpreter encounters this symbol it will ignore anything that follows it till the end of the line.

x = 59

print x    #prints the value of x

here the comment tells something that is quite obvious so it is a useless comment but the interpreter will ignore it as it precedes the # symbol. The same code can have a useful comment if written in this way

```
x = 59
```

```
print x    #prints marks of student in English
```

This is an example of a useful comment because it tells us something important about the meaning of variable x.

Comment can be of a single complete line too like in the following code

```
#this is a single line comment.
```

```
#these two lines are ignored by interpreter
```

```
x = 59
```

```
print x
```

Comments must be included in the code to increase its usability and readability.

## 3.8 getting input from the user

Up till now we have just used values assigned to the variables given by us in the code like this

Var = 34

This is known as a hard coded value. But many times the value is given by the user at run time. We need a way to get input from the user and store it in a variable. In Python there is a built in function called raw_input that will wait for the user to enter a value. When enter is pressed the interpreter resumes its function.

```
>>> input = raw_input()
Some user entered info
>>> print input
Some user entered info
```

The type of the input variable will depend upon the value given by the user as input.

# Summary

In this chapter we learnt the following concepts.

- Value is a basic unit of code like a number, a character stc.

- Variable is a name or label given to a vale so that a program can remember it for later use.

- A category of values is called its variable type.

- An expression is a combination of variables, values and operators that will amount to a single result.

- Concatenation is joining of two string values together.

- Comments are parts of a program that are ignored by the interpreter but should be used to explain parts of code.

- To get input from the user raw_input program is used.

# Chapter 4
# Conditional statements

# Chapter 4
# Conditional Statements

Up till now we have written very simple programs that work in a flow and statements are executed line by line. However, as we know programs are based on real world problems and in the real world the work flow is seldom in a single line continuum. Many times we have to check different conditions that tell us what decision to make. If the weather is cloudy take an umbrella because it may rain. Otherwise there is no need of it. If guests are coming over to stay take out the extra mattress and beddings from the attic. In both these cases the decision depends on first checking the condition. If the condition is true we take one path and if it is false, take the other path.

In computer programs also we can check statements for conditions and take a path if the condition is true and take another path if the condition is false. Such statements are called conditional statements. The result of a conditional statement is always a Boolean value either true or false. Special operators known as comparison operators are used to form conditional statements.

## 4.1 Comparison Operators

Comparison operators are almost always used in conditional statements. They compare to values and determine whether the condition is true or false. As we have mentioned earlier true and false are special type of variables in Python called bool which is short for Boolean so if we want to find the type whether true or false we write code like this

```
>>> type(True)
<type 'bool'>
>>> type(False)
        <type 'bool'>
```

The first operator is the == operator that compares whether two values are equal or not. If they are equal the result is true and if not then the result is false. For example

```
>>> result = 5==5
```

```
>>> print result
```

True

Here an important point to note is not to confuse = and ==. = is an assignment operator and is used to give a value to a variable on the other hand == is a comparison operator and is used to compare two values and return a result of a bool type.

There are a number of other comparison operators also. The following is a list of comparison operators and their functions.

```
x != y
# checks if x is not equal to y
x > y
# checks if x is greater than y
x < y
# checks if x is less than y
x >= y
# checks if x is greater than or equal to y
x <= y
# checks if x is less than or equal to y
x is y
# checks if x is the same as y
x is not y
```

#checks if x is not the same as y

All these comparison operators can work with all types of variables but their functionality might vary slightly with variable types. There is no => operator and =< operator.

## 4.2 Logical operators

We have seen how to take steps checking different conditions but what if we want to check more than one condition being true or false simultaneously. For that purpose, we use logical operators. There are three logical operators

- and

- or

- not

and will return true if all the conditions joined by and are true. Or will return true if all the conditions joined by it are true. For example,

>>> x=3

>>> result = x>0 and x<5

>>> print result

True

For the or operation check the following example

x = 5

result1 = x>0 and x<5

result2= x>0 or x<5

print result1

false

print result2

true

In this example we see that in both cases one condition is true and one is false. The expression with the and operator returns false and the expression with or operation returns true. Any non zero value is considered as true in Python so

>>>x=4

>>>result = 17 and x<10

>>>print result

True

This working of Python has some benefits and would be later illustrated. The not or negation operator is used to reverse the effect of the Boolean expression.

## 4.3 The if statement

The if statement is used to change the flow of control of the program. Based on certain condition we may want certain chunk of code to execute and certain to not execute. The if statement makes it possible. In the if condition we check whether the conditional statement is true. If it is true then we execute a certain code and if it is not true then we do not execute the code nested in the if statement.

For example, if the marks of the student are greater than 50 we print student is passed. A simple flow chart is used to depict this scenario.

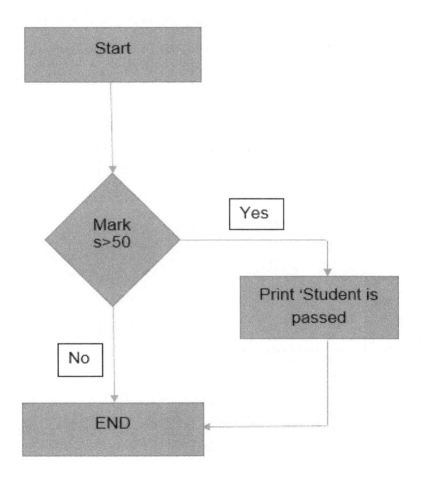

The above figure illustrates a simple case of the if statement. It can be written as follows:

Marks = 55
If marks>50:
    Print 'the student has passed'
        Here the if statement is true so the block of code nested

in it will be executed. Instead of enclosing the code nested

within an if statement in some form of brackets, Python

interpreter makes use of indentation to mark which code is

nested inside the if statement. The code that comes within the if is written after giving four blank spaces.

Here if the condition is false we are doing nothing but we can easily add an alternative code for the case when the if condition does not amount to be true.

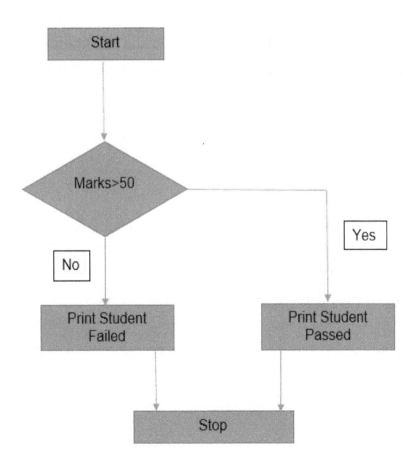

The code for above flow chart looks like this:

If marks>50:

    print 'Student Passed

else:

    print 'Student failed.'

In case of if statement either the condition will be true or false so only one flow of execution will take place. The alternate cases are known as branches. However most of the time there are more than one possibility. When there are many options and we have to choose between one of them we use chained conditions. That is when we use elif and else together with the if statement.

For example, consider a program that generates a grade depending upon student's average marks.

```
if marks >=90:
    print 'Grade A'
elif marks<90 and marks>=80:
    print 'Grade B'
elif marks<80 and marks>=70:
    print 'Grade C'
elif marks<70 and marks>=60:
    print 'Grade D'
else:
    print 'Student Failed.'
```

Elif is basically a short form of else if. In this way we can add as many conditions as required to fulfil our scenario efficiently. Only one branch is executed. If one elif condition is true, the next conditions are not checked. Only the branch that is first true will be executed. There is no limit to elif conditions. However, whenever else is used it has to be the last one. However, including else is not necessary and all the statements can be elif statements.

## 4.4 Nested if statements

Sometimes one if statement is used within another if statement. This is called the nested if scenario. The nested if is created using the proper indentation of code. For example, consider the following code

```
if x == y:
print 'x and y are equal'
else:
if x < y:
print 'x is less than y'
else:
print 'x is greater than y'
```

This is the simplest case of a nested conditional example. Here if x and y are equal first statement is executed otherwise we go inside the else condition where there are a further two branches. These branches determine whether the value of x is less than y or x is greater than y. The nested conditions become difficult to read and confusing soon so it

is recommended to avoid too many levels of nesting. Simple nesting can be avoided using logical operators. For example, consider this code

```
if 0 < x:
  if x < 1:
    print 'x is a positive single-digit number.'
```

It can be easily replaced using this code

```
if 0 < x and x < 10:
    print 'x is a positive single-digit number.'
```

# Summary

In this chapter we have learnt the following concepts

- Comparison operators are those operators that compare the value of two operands.
- Logical operators and and or are used to join more than one expression.
- The not logical operator is used to negate the expression.
- If statement is used to enable partial execution of code.
- If, elif and else are used to allow conditional execution of code.

# Chapter 5
# Functions

# Chapter 5
# Functions

Sometimes there is a piece of code that needs to be used a large number of times. For example, we want to calculate the cumulative GPA of students in a batch. Now if

there are two hundred students in a batch it will be extremely cumbersome and useless to write the same code for the whole batch of students again and again. That is where the

concept of functions come along. In functions we write a piece of code that performs a specific task. Whenever we need to do that task we call the same code. We give

a special name to the piece of code called the function name, so whenever we need to perform that specific function we call the same code by its function name.

There are a number of functions already written in Python and saved in its library. We can use them for our ease in order to avoid writing new code we reuse the code that is already written and tested for bugs. Functions can take in values as input and return some output that is the result of the computation or functionality that the function performs.

First we give some examples of built in functions and then we will move on to how we can write our own functions. There is always a need to write new functions for our specific

purposes and once you start proper coding you will find yourself writing functions all the time.

## 5.1 Built In Functions

One of the most common examples of a built in function is the type function that will tell the type of the variable or value being used. For example

```
>>> type(32)
<type 'int'>
```

The same can be done with any variable. For example,
```
>>>var = 32
type(var)
<type 'int'>
```

Here the name of the function is type so the function call will be type. Within the brackets the function takes input of a variable or value. This is known as the argument. Many functions take an argument but not all. There can be functions that do not take any arguments. Here the type function not only take in an argument but it also gives out a result or return value. It tells us the type of the variable. Just like the arguments, it is not mandatory that every function should return a value. A function may or may not return a value.

With the type function the type cast function can also be used. The cast changes the type of one variable to the other variable. Sometimes users enter values as input. We do not know which type of data the user is entering so we explicitly type cast it according to our needs so that we can store it for later use in our database and use it accordingly.

## 3.1.1 The type conversion functions

The type conversion functions are named after variable names. They take in an argument as the value that needs to be converted. The int function takes in any value and converts it into an integer.

>>>int(3.4556)

3

>>>int(4.980)

4

Here the floating point numbers are converted into integers but there is no rounding off as one would logically assume. The decimal part is simply truncated and the remaining number is stored as an integer. If we try to convert an invalid value into an integer it will not work out.

```
>>> int('Hello')
ValueError: invalid literal for int(): Hello
```

Float function converts the arguments passed into floating point format.

>>>float (3)

3.0

>>>float('3.234')

3.234

Here again an error will be thrown out if an invalid argument is passed to the function. The str function will convert the value passed into a string. This is really helpful because we can then apply the string concatenation operations in the arguments.

## 3.1.2 max, min and len functions

Let us now state some very commonly used functions whose definitions are internally provided by Python so we can freely use them whenever required without having to define them.

The max function is used to find the maximum value from a group of values given. And the min function is used to define the minimum value from a group of values.

```
>>>max(34, 45, 54,20, 13)
54
>>>min(34, 45, 54,20, 13)
```

13

Max and min functions can be used with string values also. In the string function the lower the function in alphabetical order the greater is its value so for the max function:

>>>max('Hello World')

W

>>>min('Good')

d

Here one thing to note is that if there is a blank space in the string provided the minimal value will be the blank space.

>>>min('Hello World')

' '

Another function commonly used with string is the len function which tells us the length of the string.

>>>len('HELLO WORLD')

11

Blank space is also considered as a character so it is also included in the length. The len function can only be used to find length of strings. So even if there is an integer convert it to string and then find its length

>>>len('345')

3

Sometimes in order to access a built in function we need to import its module in to program. For example, to import a random number generation function we would have to import a random library. When we call the function from this library we use the dot notation that is first the name of the library in which the function is then the function name and lastly in the braces arguments if there are any otherwise there will be empty brackets.

>>>import random

x=random.random()

Print x

Any random number would be printed on the screen. We get a floating point value between 0.0 and 1.0. we can then convert it into an integer if we want. As we are discussing the random number function here it is mandatory that we mention another concept of deterministic and non-deterministic functions. Most of the functions in computer science will always give the same value every time they are given the same input. For example, the sum function, min, max and len functions. These are called the deterministic functions because once we have seen the answer every time we enter the same values the result would be same. These are known as the deterministic functions. On the other hand, the functions that do not give the same value even when the input is same are known as non-deterministic because their outcome is not determined later. As all programs are based on algorithms so the numbers generated are not really random but that work like this. Such algorithms are called Pseudorandom algorithm.

## 3.1.3 Math functions

One group of functions that is frequently required by basic math functions like log, sin, cos, sqrt. All of these can be used by importing the math library into the program. Once the math library is imported into the program, it becomes very easy to use complex mathematical operations and solve complicated equations. Here is a demonstration of some of the basic math functions using the dot notation.

>>>import math

>>>math.sqrt(2)/2.0

0.70710678

The trigonometric functions of sin, cos, tan etc can be performed using trigonometric math operations. These functions take radians in the arguments and give the results.

```
>>> radians = 0.7
>>> height = math.sin(radians)
```

If we have degrees, we can first convert them into radians by dividing it with 360 and multiplying it with twice of pi. The value of pi can be achieved by writing math.pi. Now pi is a variable and not a function so it is written without the () brackets.

>>> degrees = 45

>>>radians= degrees/360 *2*math.pi

>>>math.sin(radians)

0.70710678

There are a number of other functions available in the math library. We can explore it through learnPython.com and other web resources.

The names of the built in functions are also reserved and while naming variables we should avoid using them as variable names. In this chapter we have learnt about the built in functions. Next let's see how we can build our own functions.

# Summary

In this chapter we learnt the following concepts.

- A function is named sequence of statements that perform a specific task.

- An argument is a value that is passed to the function as an input. A function may have zero, one or more arguments.

- A return value is an output that is generated through the function. A function may or may not have a return value.

- A function call is a statement that executes a function. It consists of the name of a function and its argument list.

- Some program or algorithm that gives the same result every time we give the same input is known as deterministic algorithm while the one that does not give the same result is known as non-deterministic.

- Flow of execution is the order in which the statements in the program run.

- A statement that reads a module file and creates a module object is known as a module statement.

- The result of the function that is passed to the main program is known as a return value. A function may or may not return a value.

# Chapter 6
# Writing your own functions

# Chapter 6
# Writing your own functions

Before we go on to learning about how to write a function let us first discuss what the benefits of writing a function are. One might argue why we should dissect the program in a disjointed sequence of statements and disturb the flow of execution.

The following is the list of main benefits of writing a function:

- It makes the program more readable and understandable. If we name a group of statements that performs a specific function, we specify their use accordingly in the function name. Now we know whenever we will call the function it will work the same function that we called.

- Functions make the program much smaller. If do not have to write the recitative code again and again. We just write it once in a function and then make the call repetitively.

- If a program is wisely divided into parts, it is much easier to debug it and find errors in it. When we know which part of program does what we just go to that part and update it whenever the need arises.

- If a program is well written and properly debugged it can be saved and then imported to be used in other programs.

The function definition is very important. It should convey the meaning as to what the function does. It should be concise and have proper meaning. For example, if there is a function that calculates the sum of some number, name it sum or calcSum. Another important thing is to decide when to divide a program into a function. Ideally a function is a unit of a program so it is supposed to do a single task. When you a generating a student transcript there should be one function that calculates the grade for individual courses, on that calculates semester GPAs and have another that calculates the cumulative GPAs atleast. Writing a function is a shrewd task and one learns with experience when to divide a program into a function and make it work.

## 6.1 Defining a function

Now let us come to the main part of defining a function. The function definition consists of the name of the function and the arguments it takes as well as the sequence of statements that the function executes. The first line of the function is known as the header and the rest of the function is called the body.

Here is a small function.

```
def print_poem():
print 'Humpty Dumpty sat on a wall'
print 'Humpty Dumpty had a great fall'
print "All the king's horses and all the King's men"
print "Couldn't put humpty together again"
```

This function, whenever called, prints the nursery rhyme Humpty Dumpty. The first line of the function 'def print_poem():' is the header of the function. The header must end in a semi colon. The name of the function is print_poem. The rules of the function name are the same as those of variable names, only capital and small letters and numbers or underscores. The name cannot begin with a number and avoid using reserved words as a name. Whenever you have used a name for a function, avoid using the same name for a variable.

Here you see the first two print statements have quotes while the last two lines have double quotes. Although single and double quotes can both be used and it is up to us to choose whichever but if there is a single quote or apostrophe within a sentence then we should use double quotes outside.

When the function ends give an empty line. The statements in a function are indented to be grouped together. It is four blank spaces before beginning the line of code. The interpreter will keep on giving an (...) elliptical until it receives an empty line. It will execute the function whenever it is called for example,

>>> print_poem()

Humpty Dumpty sat on a wall

Humpty Dumpty had a great fall

All the king's horses and all the King's men

Couldn't put humpty together again

When we define a function, a function object is created with the name we have given to it. If we print the object it gives us following information about the function.

```
>>> print print_poem
<function print_poem at 0xb7e99e9c>
>>> print type(print_poem)
    <type 'function'>
```

The type function is used to know the type of print_poem and as it states it is a type of function object. The empty parenthesis in this function definition indicates that this function takes no arguments. Now let us take a look at a function that takes arguments and returns a value.

## 6.2 Void functions, arguments and parameters

As mentioned earlier some functions give a result or an output. The output is known as a return value. But not all functions return a value like the function print_poem. So the function print_poem is a void function. A function that does not give a return value is known as a void function.

Now let us come to arguments and parameters. Consider a function that takes in three integers as arguments and returns the average of these numbers.

>>>def calc_average(val1, val2, val3):

Sum = val1+val2+val3

Avg=Sum/3

print Avg

return Avg

In this function three arguments are passed and within the function the arguments are assigned to variables val1, val2 and val3. These three variables are called parameters. Here first the average is printed on screen and then it is returned to the main flow also where it is assigned to some variable. The call will look like this

>>>average = calc_average(34,45,35)

The result of the function or return value is assigned to the variable average and that value can then be used to compute other results.

## 6.3 Writing function within functions

We can also make function calls within a function. Consider three functions that print different poems: print_humpty, print_twinkle, print_oldkingcole. These three functions print three different poems. Now if we want to print all the three poems together we write this function

>>>def print_poems():

print_humpty()

   print_twinkle()

   print_oldkingcole()

This one function print_poems consists of three function calls within it. It will print all three poems together.

## 6.4 Flow of execution

Flow of control must be kept in view while writing different functions and making the function calls. The flow of control is the order in which the statements are executed. Execution is always starting at the beginning of the program. The statements are executed one at a time, from top to the bottom. The function definition must be written before the call to the function. Function definition does not alter the flow of execution but the statements inside the function definition are not executed until the call to the function is made. Whenever the interpreter encounters a function call it jumps to the function definition and executes the statements inside the function. Then it comes back to where it left and completes the execution.

This is simple enough but when there are many function calls nested within the function calls the flow of control might become confusing to the programmer. However, for the interpreter it is easy to remember and it will not get confused, it keeps tags on where it left off and once it completes the statements within a function definition it will come back to exactly where it left off whether it is within another function or in the main program. If the function definition is not written before the function call, an error would occur as the program will not know where to go and it cannot go further below the call, as it has a tag to return to the line from where the call has been made.

Although the interpreter remembers the flow of control, it is essential that the programmer also knows about the program flow. Because the programmer has to do error control and debugging. If there is an error, it can only be caught if the programmer knows exactly where the program flow will go.

## 6.5 Debugging and exception handling

Debugging and exception handling both pertains to finding and locating errors and trying to fix them up in a neat and clean way. The main purpose is that the program must not hang or stop working. Instead a polite message is given that tells the user that something is wrong and what should be done alternatively. To do exception handling we write try and catch statements. The most common errors occur when taking input from the user. When the program is expecting one sort of input and something else is given to it to work upon. This results in breaking of program or in other words errors.

Take the example of a simple program that converts the temperatures degrees Fahrenheit into degrees Celsius. It takes degrees Fahrenheit as user input and gives out degrees Celsius as an output.

```
inp = raw_input('Enter Fahrenheit Temperature:')
fahr = float(inp)
cel = (fahr - 32.0) * 5.0 / 9.
print cel
```

Now the program is expecting a floating point value to be entered but if the user enters a string value, the following error statements can be issued.

```
Python fahren.py
Enter Fahrenheit Temperature:72
22.2222222222
Python fahren.py
Enter Fahrenheit Temperature:fred
Traceback (most recent call last):
File "fahren.py", line 2, in <module>
fahr = float(inp)
```

ValueError: invalid literal for float(): fred

The user will be completely lost if the program hangs in the middle so we do exception handling of this error like this using try and catch statements

```
inp = raw_input('Enter Fahrenheit Temperature:')
try:
fahr = float(inp)
cel = (fahr - 32.0) * 5.0 / 9.0
print cel
except:
print 'Please enter a number'
```

In this case, first the statements in the try block are executed and if all goes well the catch block is ignored. If the input entered by the user is a string value an exception occurs but instead of the program hanging up or crashing a polite message is conveyed to the user to enter a number instead of anything else. This process is known as catching an exception. The error message not only helps the user in understanding what the issue that is occurring is but it also enables the programmer to know where exactly the error had occurred and what to do about it. A program that has proper exception handling is easy to debug and update. We can incur changes in such a programs much more easily than a program that has no error handling that was done by the programmer.

Debugging provides an easy way to find logical errors. Errors that the interpreter does not have the ability to capture but they are causing errors to occur in the program and the program does not give a proper result because of them. Debugging is a way of finding such errors. In Python such errors can occur by using wrong comparison operators like <= instead of < or >= instead of >. Sometimes the programmer might accidently write – instead of + or mix up the operators which might end up causing problems. The syntax would be okay for the interpreter and it does not throw an error message but in actuality the result will be wrong because of typing errors.

In Python, indentation and spacing is also a major cause of errors and care should be taken while leaving spaces, especially in nested blocks of code.

# Summary

In this chapter we learnt the following concepts

- In addition to built in functions we can also write functions on our own that are better suited to our requirements and needs.

- The functions that we write may or may not take input values called arguments and may or may not give out a result called a return value.

- The functions that do not return a value are known as void functions.

- Inside the functions the arguments are given to variables known as parameters.

- A function call executes the statements within a function.

- The flow of control is maintained by the interpreter because it keeps tags on the places from where it leaves the execution. This gives the ability to move within a function and return to the exact same place after executing the statements within a function definition.

# Chapter 7
# Iteration or Looping

# Chapter 7
# Iterations or Looping

In the last chapter we saw how function calls make the flow of control jump from one statement to another. The original flow of control starting from the beginning of the statements to the end is known as the physical flow of control. However, the actual flow of control might differ from the physical flow of control. The actual flow of control is known as the logical flow of control while the function calls and the if statements are one way in which we can change the actual flow of control. Another way are loops or iterations. Looping enables us to execute a statement or a group of statements again and again within a continuous cycle until a certain condition is met. This helps in performing a task a number of times by just a few lines of code. When the same task needs to be repeated say a thousand number of times a computer can easily do it without tiring by using the looping statements. Before we move on to explain the structure of looping statements lets discuss an ability of Python that often comes in handy in making condition for the looping statements. It is the ability of Python to update its variable values. A variable is defined by assigning a value to it. However, it can be updated later to change the value of the variable. It can have a new value as well as its value can be updated based on its previous value. For example, consider a variable of the name x that can have any value. Defining a variable and giving it a value in known as initializing a variable. If a variable is not defined or initialized before being used Python will throw an error message stating that the variable in use has not been defined. It is important that the variable initialized before being used because it might have some garbage data stored in it that would disturb the calculations of the program.

```
x = 0
```

```
x = x+1
```

Here the value of x will be 1 after these statements. If we omit the first statement and give only the second one

```
x = x+1
```

the interpreter will throw and error. For example,

```
x = x+1
```

Nameerror: name 'x' is not defined.

This error occurs because in Python assignment statements the left hand side is evaluated before the right hand side so when it encounters x+1 it does not understand what the value x is. There are two types of variable updating statements.

X = 1

X = X+1

This is known as an increment statement.

X = 1

X = X-1

This is known as a decrement statement. Both the increment and the decrement statements are used to update the value of any variable that has been previously defined.

## 7.1 The while loop

The while statement is the main looping statement and is mostly used whenever simple iterations are required. Its structure is as follows:

Counter = 10

while counter>0:

print counter

counter = counter-1

print 'Backward counting from 10 to 1'

This simple while loop will keep on checking the while condition again and again until the condition becomes false. Until the condition becomes false, every time the cycle goes through the loop. Then after the condition becomes false the interpreter resumes the former activity and continues with the program statements just after the loop. Following diagram illustrates the flow of while controls.

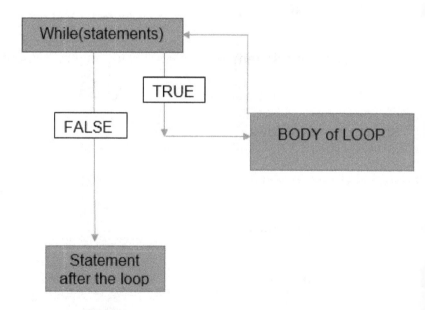

Until the loop statement is true the program will keep on rotating within the loop body. When it becomes false the program moves further away from the loop, to the statement right after the loop body. Like the other nested statements, the body of the loop is also grouped into the loop by indentation. The point at which the flow of control reaches the first statement of the loop is known as the loop entry. The point at which the loop condition is tested and the decision is made either to begin to start a new iteration or skip to the statement right after the loop is known as loop test. And the condition that causes the loop to terminate is known as the loop exit condition. It works in a way that loop termination would occur only at one point and that is when the iteration is complete and the while checks for the condition. Although the condition might be true halfway through the iteration but the iteration will be completed before the loop exit occurs.

The example that we have seen above is a type of loop called count controlled loop because is runs a specified number of times. Counter is not the only way to control the number of loop iterations. There is also an event control loop. It is a loop that terminates when something happens inside the loop body to signal that the loop should be exited. How many iterations the loop will go through is not always known. That is when the event controlled loop comes in. Its number of iterations depends upon the event occurring. For example, consider the case when user is providing some data. Until the user types a certain word or a sentence we need to keep on taking data from the user. Every time the user enters a line the loop condition checks whether the input user has given matches the word that ends the looping cycle. If the input does not match the loop ending condition it will again prompt the user to enter another line, however if the input given by the user is same as the loop ending condition, the looping cycle breaks and the flow of execution comes out of the loop going to the statement right after the loop.

In the following code example, the user can keep on enter data line. It will stop once the user writes done in the input.

```
line = 'userinput'
while line!= 'done':
    line = raw_input()
    print line
```

However, there is one small thing in this code that might be a problem. It prints the last message 'done' from the user also. If we do not want the word done to be printed

we can use the break statement within the loop. Break will make the loop stop so we do not need to test the while condition every time and can keep it true always.

```
while True:
    line = raw_input ('>')
    if(line == 'done'):
        break
    print line
```

In this program the user is prompted with an angle bracket to keep on entering an input until he types done. For example,

```
>Hello there
        Hello There
>How r you doing
        How r you doing
>I think I will stop now
        I think I will stop now
>done
```

Here is what a simple cycle of this program will look like. Besides the break statement there is another statement 'continue' that changes the course of iteration of a loop. Continue statement breaks the current iteration and begins a new iteration. It is different from the break statement because the break statement comes out of the loop but the continue statement begins a new iteration.

Here is a simple example of continue statement. It is the same as the previous example with a simple change. It will print all the lines of input from the users except if the user begins a line with an asterix *.

```
while True:
    line = raw_input('>')
    if line[0] == '*'
        continue
    if line == 'done'
        break
    print line
```

A simple sequence demonstrating this example is as follows

>Hello world

Hello world

>*password don't print this

>now print this

Now print this

>done

## 7.2 Infinite Loops

Whenever we talk about loops there is always a discussion about infinite loops too. A loop that does not terminate ever is known as an infinite loop.

103

```
x = 0

While True:

    x = x+1

    print x
```

This loop will keep on printing numbers forever without ever stopping. It is not a good idea to run this program because it will cause the computer to hang until the battery dies or shuts down the computer forcefully. We should always take care that the loop condition will fail at some point and the loop comes to an end. If the loop is infinite your program will hang up the entire system.

## 7.3 The for loop

The for is another way of looping in Python. The while loop is known as the indefinite loop because we do not know when the loop condition will be fulfilled and we would be able to move to the statement next to the loop. On the other hand, for is known as the definite loop. It is used to develop loops where there is a definite list of items through which we can iterate through. We have not covered the topic of lists and arrays yet but for the sake of a clear and simple example consider a list of colors as a variable.

colors = ['red', 'blue', 'green', 'yellow, 'orange']

print 'Choose one color from the list.'

for color in colors:

    print 'Option', color

print 'done'

Here color is a loop variable that automatically starts with the first item in the colors list and loops through the last item. After every loop cycle it will automatically move to the next list item, until there are no items left in the list. There is no need to manually update the loop counter in the case of a for loop. A cycle through this loop will yield following result

Choose one color from the list

Option red

Option blue

Option green

Option yellow

Option orange

Done

So for and in are reserved words and color and colors are variables.

## 7.4 Some commonly used loop functions

Loops are usually used to perform a myriad of functions but here we discuss some most commonly used loop functions. Loops are used to find the number of items in a list or to find the sum of all the items in the list.

Here is a simple program that uses the for loop to count the number of items in a list.

```
list = [32,54,65,76,12,34,56]

count = 0

for everyitem in list:

    count = count+1

print 'total items in the list are:', count
```

This program will put an increment in the value of count for every item and in the end when the list is exhausted the count will contain the total number of items in the list. With a slight variation we can make this program to calculate the sum of total number of items in the list.

```
list = [32,54,65,76,12,34,56]

count = 0

for everyitem in list:

    count = everyitem+count

print 'total items in the list are:', count
```

Now in this program we have made just one slight change and its whole functionality is changed. Every item which is our loop variable contains the value of every list item in the list so in each cycle we keep on adding the value of items to the value of count which was 0 in the beginning to make it work. It is very important in both cases to initialize the value of the count to 0 in the beginning.

Another task that is commonly done on loops are to find the greatest and smallest value in the list of the loop. Before we give that function let us introduce the None constant. None is a constant in Python that we can assign to any variable that we do not want to initialize to 0 because a 0 might make our calculations inaccurate.

val = None

list = [3,4,6,2,9,0,10]

for item in list:

    if val==None or item>val

```
val=item

print 'Loop:', item, val

print 'Largest item is ',  val
```

a pass through this code will yield the following results

Loop: 3,3

Loop: 4,4

Loop: 6,6

Loop: 2,6

Loop: 9,9

Loop: 0,9

Loop: 10,10

Largest item is 10

The same program can be written for the smallest value by just changing the > sign to the < sign. This program works for negative numbers also because we have initialized val to None instead of 0.

```
val = None

list = [3,4,6,2,9,0,10]

for item in list:

    if val==None or item<val

        val=item

    print 'Loop:', item, val

print 'Smallest item is ', val
```

This program now will find the smallest value in the list. Although the length and sum of the lists can also be found by using built in functions of len() and sum() but it is better that when you are beginning to learn the language you do these small exercises on your own to learn the syntax and logic behind the built in function. We have provided the examples using the for loop, now try to make the same work for while loop. Although logically for such operations for loop is more suited and should always be preferred.

# Summary

In this chapter we learnt the following concepts

- A loop is a way to do the same task repetitively many number of times.

- A counter is a variable that calculates the number of times within a loop.

- A loop will end when the terminating condition is met.

- A loop that does not have a terminating condition is known as an infinite loop.

- There are two main types of loops for loop and while loop.

- For loop is known as definite loop and the while loop is known as indefinite loop.

# Conclusion

Thank you again for purchasing this book!

I hope that this book was able to help you. However, there is still a long way to go to master the art of programming in Python. This book must have introduced you to the world of programming in general and Python especially. The next step from here is to read advanced concepts like files, dictionaries and networking concepts.

Remember that the key to master any language is practice, practice and practice. The more you work on the language the more you will learn. Use online help forums extensively while working.

Finally, if you enjoyed this book, then I'd like to ask you for a favor, would you be kind enough to leave a review for this book on Amazon? It would be greatly appreciated! Please feel free to give your honest opinions as this could help me make improvements.

Thank you and good luck!

www.ingramcontent.com/pod-product-compliance
Lightning Source LLC
Chambersburg PA
CBHW071224050326
40689CB00011B/2440